PAINTING WITH LIGHT

F. William Sunderman Sr.

Sunderman, F. William
    Painting With Light / F. William Sunderman.
    1st edition
    ISBN 0–9632927–1–4

Library of Congress Catalog Card Number: 93–78236

This limited first edition of
PAINTING WITH LIGHT
has been privately printed,
and personally signed by
F. William Sunderman Sr., M.D., Ph.D., Sc.D.

J. William Sunderman,

To the Library of
Jefferson Medical College.

For the invaluable help of my beloved Martha–Lee who urged that some of my exhibition prints of previous years be collated, I make grateful acknowledgment.

PREFACE

My real interest in photography began while serving as an intern at The Pennsylvania Hospital on the service of Dr. George W. Norris, Professor of Medicine at the University of Pennsylvania. During ward rounds one morning, Dr. Norris made an offhand remark that a photograph of the patient we were examining would make an appropriate addition for insertion in the revised edition of his book on *Physical Diagnosis* (Norris and Landis). This remark prompted me to purchase a second hand Korona View camera with a f 4.5 Turner–Reich lens, ground glass back, a stable tripod, and a black cape, as well as developing and enlarging equipment. During my internship, scores of medical photographs were processed. I still retain my Korona View camera and am pleased to note that several of the prints in this volume were obtained through the use of this faithful instrument, which I have possessed for 70 years. The other prints were obtained with Speedgraphic, Rolliflex, and Leica cameras.

Throughout my medical career, I have maintained an active interest in two hobbies, – playing chamber music (my primary spare time activity) and black and white photography with airbrushing. Following the recent revised publication of *Musical Notes of a Physician*, I was urged to assemble into book form a reproduction of some of my prints that through the years have won awards at national and international exhibitions as well as acceptance in art museums. As a consequence, I have selected such prints for insertion in this volume. It might be noted that the original prints are larger(16 x 20) and harbor a more precise range of black and white tones.

F. W. S.

All Art is but the imitation of Nature.
Lucius Annaeus Seneca
8 B.C. – 65 A.D.

Nature is the art of God.
Sir Thomas Browne
1605–1682

TABLE OF CONTENTS

PAINTING WITH LIGHT*

Emerson, when he was asked why he took up the studies of geology and chemistry in his more mature years, replied that he did so in order to make himself a better poet. Most of us need outlets in hobbies, and I have always taken the position that a man should never be called upon to defend or justify them for, otherwise, they would cease to be hobbies.

The beginner in photography soon realizes that photography is many–sided. It satisfies the urge to create something and, above all, to preserve bright bits of life which we feel are slipping so swiftly past. Moreover, the technique of photography can be made quite simple, requiring no especial talent, or it can be as difficult as one chooses to make it.

The appeals of photography are many–sided. Certain individuals will be attracted by the mechanical side of photography, – the so–called gadgeteers with their fl.2 lenses and their 1/10,000 second shutter mechanisms. Others will get a thrill dabbling in the dark room, working with developing formulas and toners. I believe that most photographic enthusiasts, however, really want to make pictures, and they yearn to render prints of good quality, fine texture, and sound composition. Finally, there is a group of photographers who are attracted to photography primarily as an art and not as a craft. This group is interested in creating pictures that will endure and that can be projected and appreciated in the future beyond the lifetime of the maker. It is my belief that most amateur photographers would really, deep in their hearts, like to achieve recognition in this group.

---

* Adapted from an address given at a meeting of the combined camera clubs of Philadelphia and vicinity, circa 1950.

To enter the "true art" group, one must be able to produce something of intense emotional appeal. Until a picture can arouse some strong emotional reaction, it cannot be properly classified as true art. Prints in the category to which I refer are beyond the realm of the usual competitive salon adventures. To have a print accepted in a recognized salon, it must have meritorious technical qualities; however, it is regrettable that the subject matter of an accepted print does not necessarily always possess that evasive aesthetic quality that goes to make up works of art. There is much justification in the position taken by many of our prominent art critics that the great majority of prints accepted in our present–day international salons are prints that are very short–lived and might properly be classified as "calendar art."

Several years ago, I attended one of the many international salon exhibitions and became interested in watching how eventually almost everyone's attention become focused on one outstanding print among the 200 or 300 exhibited. The viewers would walk about the exhibit but would eventually return for a second admiration of one of the prints which was entitled *Spring* and made by the late, great Belgian engineer and pictorialist, Missone. On viewing this picture, one could not refrain from exclaiming how beautiful it really was. With all the differences of opinions, almost everyone will eventually agree upon one or two prints in a large exhibition as being outstanding and possessing that aesthetic quality which will live and which might be termed "true art."

Pictorial photography has often been referred to as *painting with light*. To know how to see is probably one of the most essential requirements for photography. We seem to be blind artistically, and our eyes need considerable education to enable us to see photographically.

Let me give you an example of what I mean. Sometime ago, I noticed a mortar and pestle placed in a dark corner beneath one of my laboratory tables. Being in shadow, it appeared nearly black. I asked one of my technicians (partly in order to call her attention to the fact that the mortar and pestle should have been put into the proper cabinet) what color did the mortar and pestle look like to her. She replied somewhat in astonishment, "Why it looks white. It's a mortar and pestle, isn't it?" Now this was the reply of reason and experience, but it was not really what she saw. Although the mortar and pestle appeared as dark gray in the shadows, nevertheless, since mortar and pestles are made of white porcelain, she replied by thinking and not by seeing.

If one watches the children playing bareheaded in the streets against the light, one will see their heads surrounded by a shining halo. Now stop anyone and ask what those heads look like, and you will be told that they are either red, brown, blond, or black. Ask them if they see anything else, and they will be astonished to find that they do not. Now show them the same picture on the ground glass of a view camera and then, when distracting side views are eliminated and the views are reduced in size, they will be amazed at the beautiful halo and probably tell you what a marvelous mechanical device the camera really is.

Many of us find it difficult to realize that there are two types of vision, – that of the eye and that of reason. Contrary to what one might expect of primitive peoples, they do not see with their eyes but according to their experience and reason. To learn to see with one's eyes, in the sense in which I mean, requires patient effort and endeavor.

In order to take pictures that appeal, some attention must be paid to composition. There are many individuals who feel that proficiency in pictorial composition is in some way related to a mysterious sixth sense. This is far from the actual facts, since pictorial composition can be very readily learned and a proficiency acquired. It is not a precisely memorized subject of study but becomes developed more or less into an unconscious reflex as, for example, driving a car.

I feel that perhaps it might not be too elemental to mention briefly some of the fundamental reasons underlying the principles of composition. Of course, in photography, just as in music or literature, there are certain rebellious spirits who hold to the opinion that there should be absolute freedom in composition and that anything is alright provided you really want to do it that way. Now the idea of absolute freedom is a fascinating thought, and I have often pondered upon it. The fact remains, however, that if one really wants to have pictures, music, or stories get over to other individuals, one has to comply with certain more–or–less definite rules. In photography, just as in writing stories or composing music, one has to adhere to certain customs with which ones' associates are accustomed to understand, if the message is to get across. In this sense, pictorial composition is more–or–less the basis of making a picture in the manner that people *have agreed to like or in a manner which they understand.* As a result of years of observations and experiences, people have arbitrarily established certain conventions, and they demand that we observe these restrictions.

Photography, like all graphic arts, is symbolic. The most photographic photograph of a house really doesn't look like a house. To anyone who is not trained to recognize the symbols, it really doesn't resemble a house. It is merely an arrangement of tones from black to white on a plane surface that we have learned to recognize as representing a house. Every race has developed its own set of symbols differing from those of other races, yet more or less alike. For example, it is a customary requirement of oriental art that there be no empty spaces and that every part of the picture be filled. Thus, the code of arrangements as well as the code of symbols varies from time to time, from country to country, and is subject to many modifications. We must adhere to the code that is acceptable and understood by the individuals from whom we wish to receive appreciation.

As a result of many years of study, Poore found that most pictures, which have stood the test of time and are of proved sound composition, according to our European and American viewpoints, may be reduced in their broad, general lines to a number of basic geometric forms with variations and combinations. Seven of Poore's forms are shown on the figure.* In my opinion, the beginner might do well to plan pictures with geometric forms loosely in mind.

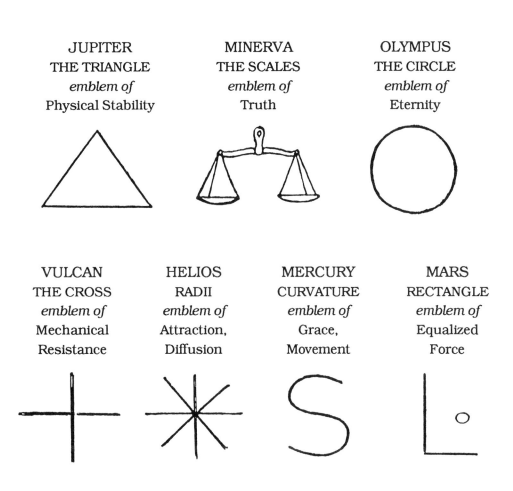

JUPITER	MINERVA	OLYMPUS
THE TRIANGLE	THE SCALES	THE CIRCLE
emblem of	*emblem of*	*emblem of*
Physical Stability	Truth	Eternity

VULCAN	HELIOS	MERCURY	MARS
THE CROSS	RADII	CURVATURE	RECTANGLE
emblem of	*emblem of*	*emblem of*	*emblem of*
Mechanical	Attraction,	Grace,	Equalized
Resistance	Diffusion	Movement	Force

* Adapted from Poore, Henry Rankin: *Art's Place in Education.* New York, G.P. Putnam's Sons, 1937, p. 59.

Also, I should like to suggest that the beginner copy scenes that appeal to him or her. No two pictures can be made precisely alike, and there is much to be gained by taking a photograph of a scene previously taken by a recognized master. It is said that Sheila Kay Smith learned how to write literature by actually coping Thomas Hardy in an effort to acquire style. The great immortal Brahms did not hesitate to use the theme of Wagner's *Prize Song* as the opening theme in his beautiful *A Major Violin Sonata.* In this, I am reminded of the professor who advised his students that if they copied one book, that was plagiarism; but if they copied five books, that was research.

I adhere strongly to the view that pictures are made and not taken. To me, it does not make an iota of difference how the picture was made and what process was employed. It is the final result that counts. Ysaye, the famous Belgian violinist, used to tell his pupils that he didn't care if they played their violins with their toes, just so long as the music they played sounded well.

Individual tastes in photography vary tremendously. One person may want every line sharply defined; another may want the picture diffused. Some individuals will prefer to make still–lifes, while others may regard still–lifes as the bunk. But whatever ones' taste may be, almost all will agree when viewing a group of prints that occasionally one print will contain subject matter which has an evasive, aesthetic quality and which appeals basically to our emotions. That picture will probably live.

F. W. S.

Architecture, sculpture, painting, music, and poetry
may truly be called the efflorescence of civilized life.
Herbert Spencer
1829–1903

Early Clinical Science

F. William Sunderman

"LET THEN our first act every morning be to make the following resolve for the day:

I shall not fear any one on earth;

I shall fear only God;

I shall not bear ill will towards anyone;

I shall conquer untruth by truth;

And in resisting untruth

I shall put up with suffering."

—Mahatma Gandhi

J. P. Taylor, analyst

F. William Sunderman

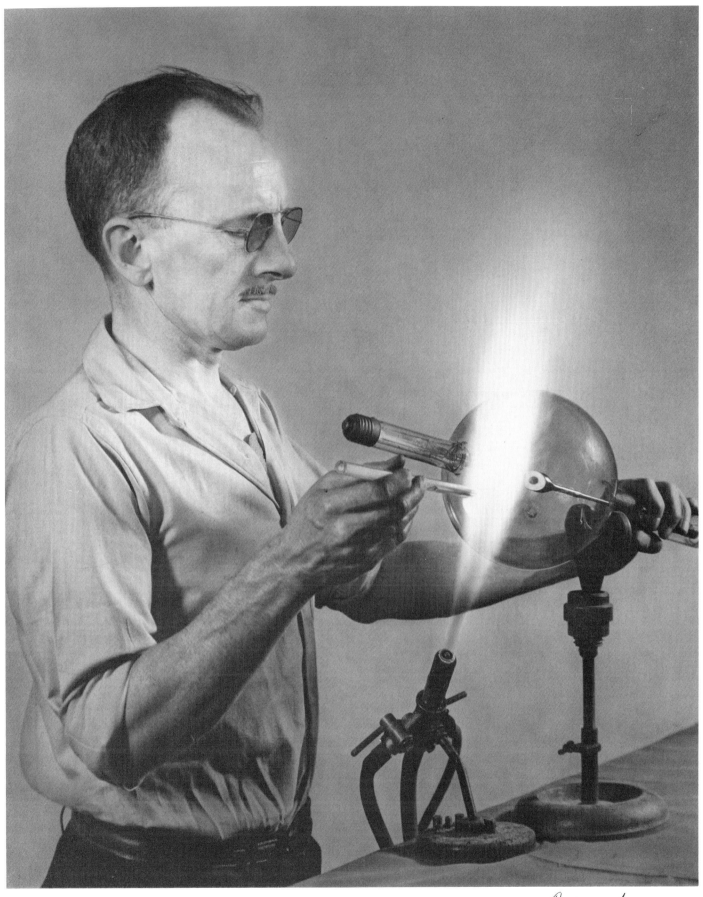

Jimmy Graham, the glass blower

F. William Sunderman

Ancestral Church (circa 991 A.D.)

 isten to the church bell's solemn toll
And ponder its ancient stately role;
May it ring out the thousand years of strife,
May it ring in a lasting peaceful life.

F. W. S.

Wedding Bells in May, 1980

J. William Sunderman

St. James, Sandys, Bermuda

 IOUS PILGRIM JOIN THE FOLD
A SACRED MAJESTY BEHOLD,
MIDST AZURE SKY AND SHINING SEA
TO PONDER ON LIFE'S DESTINY.

F. W. S.

VI

St. Clair

J. William Sunderman

Build thee more stately
mansions O my soul

— Holmes

This photograph won 1st prize in the Eastman Kodak Company's annual exhibition of pictorial photography and also 1st prize in the AMA's art exhibit. A 16 x 20 enlargement was obtained by the Art Museum in Rome for exhibition purposes.

Peace on Earth

VIII

Meditation

When Day Is Done and Shadows Fall

That Men May Live as Brothers

J. William Sunderman

Soft shadows fall through misty morn,
majestic mounts cathedrals form.
O God of mercy, hear us pray
for peace on earth this Christmas day.

F. W. S.   XI

Petition

F. William Sunderman

With appreciation for medical advancements in ages past,
With gratitude for scientific achievements that will last,
With faith in discoveries that the future may herald,
Lord, further our search for a disease–less world.

F. W. S.

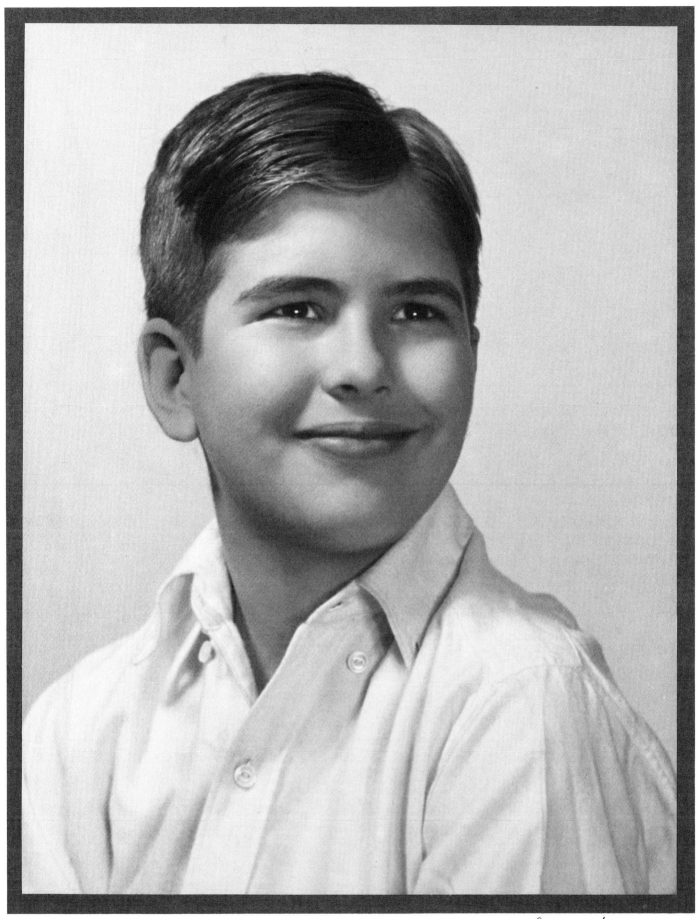

Bill Jr.

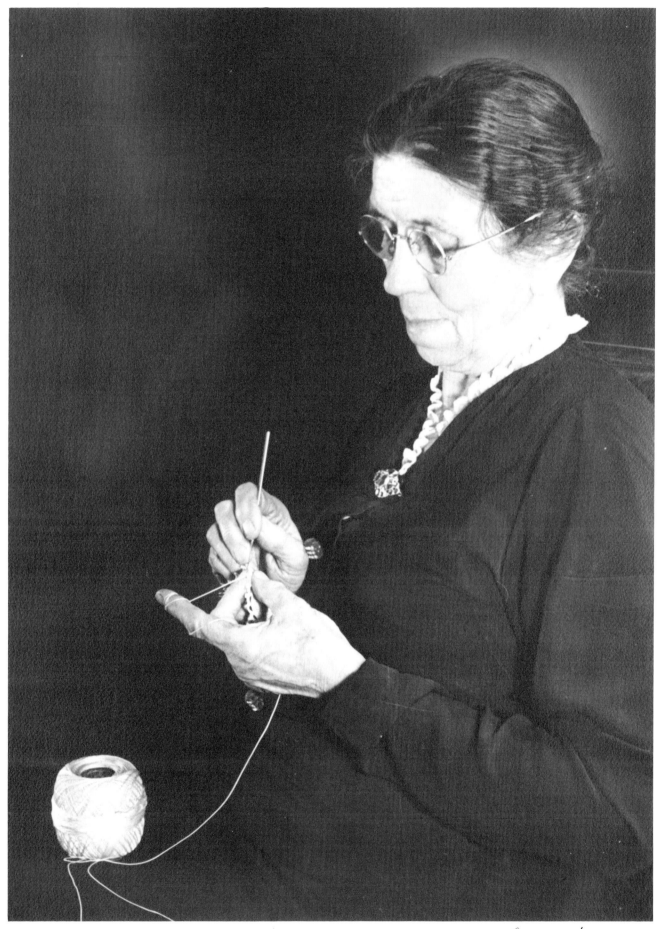

My mother, Elizabeth Lehr Sunderman

F. William Sunderman

XIV

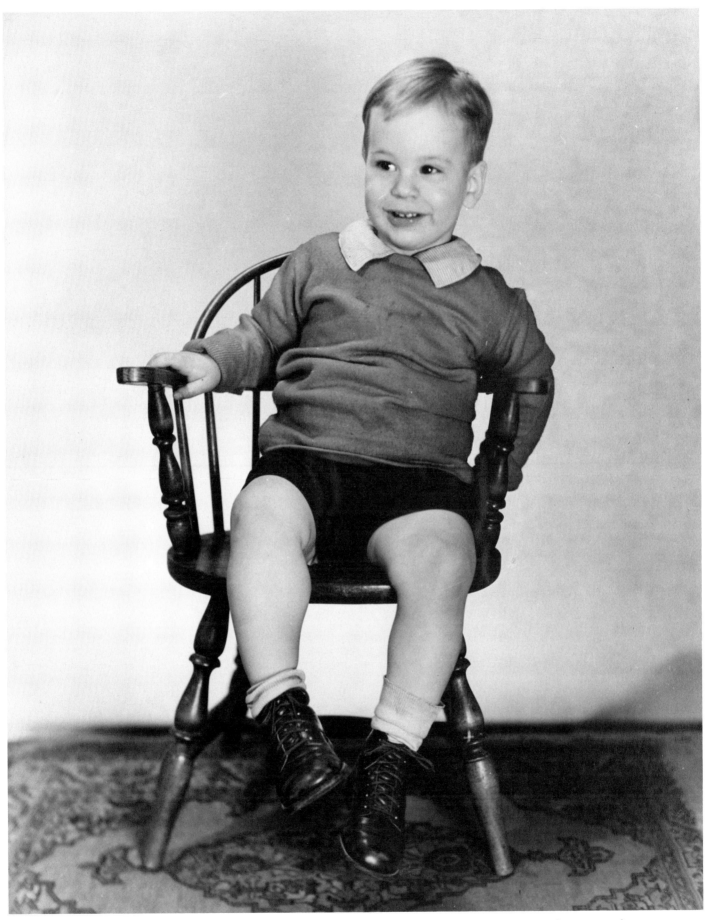

Joel

Young Piscatorian

F. William Sunderman

Joel Baily Sunderman (1944–1966)

Teach me thy way, O Lord
PSALM XXVII, 11

Self Portrait

XVIII

Clara Louise Sunderman (1900–1972)

F. William Sunderman

Tɪᴍᴇ, silent keeper of memories of tender loveliness and precious beauty, enshrine unending years with the grace and charm of her nobility.

F. W. S.

Doctors Austin, Krumbhaar, and Pepper were members of the same class in medical school. They graduated June 17, 1908, University of Pennsylvania.

The College of Physicians of Philadelphia, 1940

| J. Harold Austin | Edward B. Krumbhaar | O. H. Perry Pepper |
| Secretary | President | Vice President |

Mei Chen

J. William Sunderman

Doctor Nylan

F. William Sunderman

Peasant Madonna

F. William Sunderman

"Monk" Farinholt

Division 8, OSRD, WW II

Charlotte

F. William Sunderman

8th and Race Streets

F. William Sunderman

Kramer, the Blacksmith, at His Forge

Sparks a flying,
Happiness abounding,
Anvil resounding,
The nobility of his craft.

F. William Sunderman

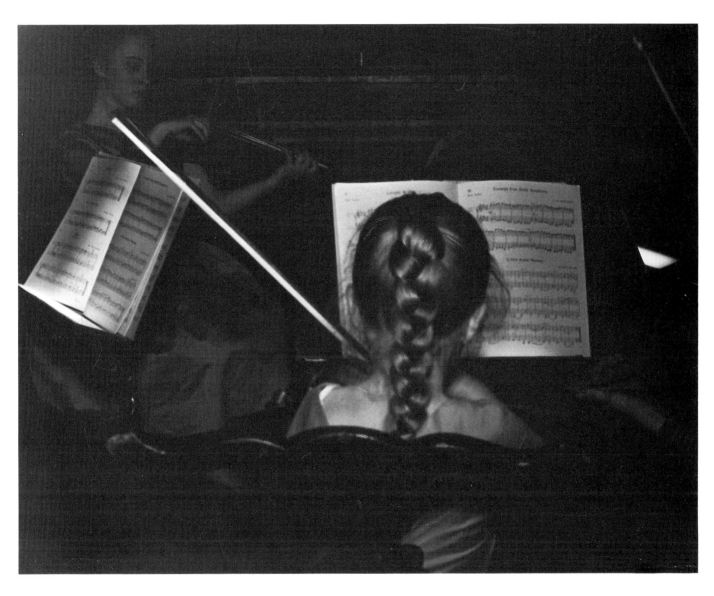

 DE TO VIOLS

Angelic sounds of thy music pervade the world.
The celestial wand was made to vibrate thy strings;
The moon to light the beauty of thy contours.
The stars of heaven are but a canopy
To frame the loveliness of thy song.
All the mysteries of nature
Are but symbols of thy soul.

F. William Sunderman

Tanya

J. William Sunderman

Euphrosyne was included in the Eastman Kodak exhibit at the New York World's Fair. This was the only nude exhibited at the Fair.

Euphrosyne

Before the Footlights

F. William Sunderman

The Austin Organ Company built the five manual organ for the exhibition at The Sesquicentennial Exposition in Philadelphia in 1926. The organ was donated by Cyrus Curtis to the University of Pennsylvania and installed in the Irvine Auditorium in 1928.

Dr. Morrison Boyd at the Curtis Organ

J. William Sunderman

Pennsylvania Farm

If Winter Comes...
Can Spring be far behind?

Gyrfalcon

J. William Sunderman

Birch Run

F. William Sunderman

Sunbeams on Winter Snow,
   Gleaming in golden glow,
      Proclaim to sleeping flora beneath

The countless years that are bequeathed.

F. W. S.

Exhortation of the Dawn

J. William Sunderman

ook to this Day! It is Life.
In its brief course lie all the
Verities and Realities of Existence.
Yesterday is but a Dream, and
Tomorrow is only a Vision.
But Today well lived
Makes every Yesterday a Dream of Happiness;
And every Tomorrow, a Vision of Hope.

from Sanscrit

Cape May

At Daybreak!
Cascades of light on ships at sea,
Resounding waves 'gainst lonely piers,
Reveal to man life's frailty
'Midst boundless skies and endless years.

F. W. S.

Dominus Illuminatio Mea

The Lord is my Light

Psalm 27.1

Incense Trail, Yemen

Commiphora myrrh

Boswellia carterii

Frankincense –(*Boswellia carterii*) gum from shrub.

Myrrh – (*Commiphora myrrh*) exudate from thorny tree

Yemen

Opening their treasures,
they presented gifts of Gold,
Frankincense and Myrrh.

Matthew 2:11

Moonlight on the Chesapeake

F. William Sunderman

Galapagos   *February, 1990*   *F. William Sunderman*

 ilent and watchful the steep crags lay
Keeping the calm in Galapagos bay,
Stirred neither creature, bush, nor flower,
All lulled to rest in the twilight hour.

And then the song of a bird rose joyous and clear
To give assurance for all to hear,
Pray, listen to the story it fain would tell,
"God's in His heaven and all is well."   *F. W. S.*

Antarctic Expedition   F. William Sunderman

 n awesome solitude, great Temples fend
The sacred fanes in frigid clime;
Symbolic of the soul's undying faith
In Life,—a miracle without end,
And Love,—a mystery without time.

F. W. S.

Toil in Poland

ENERGY of man and beast,
of earth and stream,
supports us all.
'Tis God's indestructible gift
for life and happiness.

F.W.S.

...anley, Falkland Islands, South Atlantic Ocean   F. William Sunderman

Sailing to cold and lonely isles,
After leaving rigorous toil,
Spirits are refreshed by natives' smiles
Upon landing on Falkland soil.

F. W. S.

St. David's Light, Bermuda

F. William Sunderman

Behold Saint David's towering light
That guides the ships that pass by night.
As we set sail on seas of life,
Amid the stress of storm and strife,
May our Creator's heavenly light
Guide us to our haven.   *F. W. S.*

Seven Sisters

F. William Sunderman

East River Drive, Fairmount Park

F. William Sunderman

A Farm Cathedral

 eap high the wintry festal towers

of stately basilicas on land,

Cradles for refection and power,

Gifts from God's own hand.

F. W. S.

Springtime in Green Lane

F. William Sunderman

Wicker Mart — New Orleans

F. William Sunderman

Peregrine Falcon

F. William Sunderman

The Haymakers

F. William Sunderman

Love the **work** that thou
hast learned
...and be content therewith.

– Marcus Aurelius

NOTES

about the

AUTHOR

M. L. S.

F. William Sunderman Sr., M.D., Ph.D., Sc.D.

ABSTRACT*

Dr. F. William Sunderman Sr. is a world–renowned physician, pathologist, clinical scientist, chemist, toxicologist, author, editor, photographer, and a life–long violinist. He was a pioneer in the development of clinical chemistry in the United States. He developed methods for the quantitative measurements of various chemical components of body fluids, the colligative properties of body fluids, and the metabolism of electrolytes in health and disease. His book, *Normal Values in Clinical Medicine* (Sunderman and Boerner), was widely used for may years for reference purposes. His research studies in more recent years have been focused on the toxicology of trace metals, and particularly to nickel and nickel carbonyl, and to the development of an antidote from lethal exposure.

Dr. Sunderman was born in Altoona, Pennsylvania, where he attended public schools and graduated from Juniata High School as valedictorian of his class. He graduated from Gettysburg College in 1919 and from the University of Pennsylvania School of Medicine in 1923. That began a long association with The Pennsylvania Hospital as an intern in medicine and surgery, assistant physician, and physician to the Hospital during the years of 1923 to 1947. During that period he was director of the chemistry division of the Ayer Clinical Laboratory and chief of the Diabetic and Metabolic Clinic A. In 1929 he received a Ph.D. degree in physical chemistry from the University of Pennsylvania. Dr. Sunderman returned to The Pennsylvania Hospital in 1988 as honorary pathologist and Director of the Institute for Clinical Science. He is currently Honorary Clinical Professor of Medicine at Thomas Jefferson University School of Medicine and Professor Emeritus of Pathology and Laboratoy Medicine at Hahnemann University School of Medicine. His academic honors include membership in Phi Beta Kappa, Alpha Omega Alpha, and Sigma Xi honorary societies. He is certified by the American Board of Internal Medicine, the American Board of Pathology , and the American Board of Clinical Chemists. Dr. Sunderman served for many years as an examiner for the American Board of Pathology and is life trustee of the Board.

In the field of medicine, Dr. Sunderman has been a professor in four of the five medical colleges in Philadelphia (University of Pennsylvania, Temple University, Thomas Jefferson University, and Hahnemann University). He has held similar positions at The Cleveland Clinic, the University of Texas, and Emory University where he was professor of clinical medicine and chief of clinical pathology at the Center for Disease Control (CDC). Dr. Sunderman is recognized as the Father of Proficiency Testing (or quality control) with his founding and directing the Proficiency Test Service, a monthly self–audit and advisory service subscribed to by more than 2,000 hospital and clinical laboratories in the United States and Canada. The service, founded in 1949, was the first of its kind. It continued uninterrupted for 36 years until the service was purchased by the American Society of Clinical Pathologists (ASCP). He is also known as the Father of Continuing Medical Education since he organized and directed the first workshop in this country in clinical chemistry on the topic of clinical hemoglobinometry for the ASCP in 1954 and then organized and directed a joint conference of the ASCP and the Royal Army Medical College on the same topic in London in 1955.

During World War II, Dr. Sunderman was medical director of Division 8 of the Office of Scientific Research and Development which was affiliated with the Manhattan Project at Los Alamos, New Mexico. There is a piece of the first atomic bomb explosion from Alamagorda encased in lucite sitting in his music room. Years later, again working as a medical scientific consultant with the National Aeronautics and Space Administration (NASA), he watched Alan Shepperd roar into space and into history in a Mercury space capsule atop a Redstone rocket.

Dr. Sunderman has received awards and citations from the War Department; the Department of the Navy; the Armed Forces Institute of Pathology; the American Society of Clinical Pathologists of which he is a past president; the College of American Pathologists of which he is the only surviving founding governor; the Association of Clinical Scientists of which he is the founder, a past president, and still, from its inception in 1949, the director of education; the American Association for Clinical Chemistry in 1981 for his "outstanding contributions to clinical chemistry in education"; the Japanese government for his work in saving the lives of approximately 200 workmen who were accidentally poisoned by nickel carbonyl; the International Union of Pure

---

This abstract served as the basis of the citation for the Ehrenzeller Award of The Pennsylvania Hospital presented to Dr. Sunderman on May 15, 1993.

8

and Applied Chemistry for his "life–time contributions to and promotion of nickel toxicology"; the Federal Republic of Germany in 1989 when he received the Distinguished Service Cross, Order of Merit; the Joint Congresses of the National Spanish Society of Clinical Chemistry, the International Congress of Therapeutic Drug Monitoring and Toxicology, and the International Congress on Automation and New Technology for his "Life–time Achievement in Clinical Chemistry"; and the dedication by the Governor of Bermuda of the Sunderman Seminar Room at the Bermuda Biological Station for Research where Dr. Sunderman is a life trustee. He is listed in most of the *Who's Who* including *Who's Who in the World,* and *International Who's Who in Music.*

As an author, Dr. Sunderman has written approximately 350 papers, starting in 1925, and 44 books. Three of his books are translated into Japanese and one into Italian. Also included are two non–medical books, *Our Madeira Heritage* and *Musical Notes of a Physician.* He has also been the editor of *Annals of Clinical and Laboratory Science* since its inception 23 years ago.

Dr. Sunderman has been active on the Board of Trustees of Gettysburg College, where he has served as its Chairman and is now an Honorary Life Trustee. He has founded the Sunderman Foundation for Chamber Music at Gettysburg College which presents free chamber music concerts at the College during the academic year.

Over the years Dr. Sunderman has travelled to 175 different countries. In the past 15 years, he has visited the scientific stations in Antarctica, the deserts and mountains of Yemen, and the Galapagos Islands. He lectured at the Medical University in Beijing during the Tien' Amin Square disturbances.

It should be noted that during all these many years, Dr. Sunderman has been playing his violin and playing string quartets with amateur and professional friends all over the world. He still travels throughout the United States and to England, Germany, Austria, and Italy to play chamber music. Last February, he and his son, Dr. F. William Sunderman Jr, who is chairman of the departments of laboratory medicine and pharmacology at the University of Connecticut Medical School, played together in a concert at Carnegie Hall, New York. He never travels without his violin – or his wife, Martha–Lee. And he plans never to retire.

This photograph of Dr. Sunderman in his 95th year was taken during a recent sojourn at the Bermuda Biological Station for Research (1993).